Math in My World

Math in the Backyard

By William Amato

Children's Press®
A Division of Scholastic Inc.
New York / Toronto / London / Auckland / Sydney
Mexico City / New Delhi / Hong Kong
Danbury, Connecticut

Photo Credits: Cover and all photos by Maura Boruchow
Contributing Editor: Jennifer Silate
Book Design: Laura Stein

Library of Congress Cataloging-in-Publication Data

Amato, William.
Math in the backyard / by William Amato.
        p. cm. — (Math in my world)
Includes index.
Summary: Photos and simple text illustrate the use of math while playing backyard
        bowling or eating cookies.
ISBN 0-516-23941-4 (lib. bdg.) — ISBN 0-516-23596-6 (pbk.)
1. Mathematics—Juvenile literature. [1. Mathematics.] I. Title.

QA40.5 .A527 2002
513—dc21

                                                            2001042354

Contents

Hi, my name is Kristy.

We are playing in
the **backyard.**

The three of us
are **bowling.**

There are four balls.

We each take one ball.

How many balls are left?

There is only one ball left.

Let's bowl!

I bowl first.

I try to **knock** down
all ten **pins**.

11

I knocked down six pins.

How many pins are left?

13

There are four pins left.

I hope that I can knock them down this time!

14

Mom brings us some cookies.

17

John takes two cookies.

Brian also takes two cookies.

How many cookies are left for me?

19

There are two cookies left for me.

I like playing in the backyard!

New Words

backyard (**bak**-yard) a place behind a house

bowling (**bohl**-ihng) a game in which balls are rolled at pins

knock (**nahk**) to hit something

pins (**pihnz**) bottle-shaped objects used in bowling

To Find Out More

Books

Pigs at Odds: Fun with Math and Games
by Amy Axelrod
Simon & Schuster Trade

Ten Times Better
by Richard Michelson
Marshall Cavendish Corporation

Web Site
A+ Math
http://www.aplusmath.com
Play fun games while learning about math on this Web site.

Index

About the Author

William Amato is a teacher and writer living in New York City.

Reading Consultants

Kris Flynn, Coordinator, Small School District Literacy, The San Diego County Office of Education

Shelly Forys, Certified Reading Recovery Specialist, W.J. Zahnow Elementary School, Waterloo, IL

Sue McAdams, Former President of the North Texas Reading Council of the IRA, and Early Literacy Consultant, Dallas, TX